INTO THE ARK

INTO THE ARK

BY

HANNAH T. WRIGHT
&
MARK O. VOGEL

ISBN 978-0-9915258-3-6

Layout/Text Design: Michael Laney, Mark O. Vogel

Bible Translation: Hannah T. Wright

Photographs: Mark O. Vogel

Printed in Seoul, Korea by We SP Corp. Ltd
February 2017
68407-0

Publisher: MOVimages LLC

Cover Page: Giraffe Pair, June 2010

Bible passages are translated from the KING JAMES VERSION BIBLE, and are simplified for age appropriateness.

To purchase prints of images featured in this book, please visit www.movimages.com

Don't Be In The Dark About the Ark!

Did you know… even though the Bible doesn't tell us how long Noah spent building the ark, we do know it probably took a long time! After all, the Ark was 450 feet long, 75 feet wide and 50 feet high and it had three floors!

Did you know… that the flood was the first time it had ever rained on the earth. Before the flood, God took care of the plants and animals with a mist that rose up from the ground.

Did you know… Noah was already 600 years old when the flood began!

Did you know… when God flooded the earth, it rained for forty days and nights, and the floodwaters remained for 150 days after that!

Did you know… Noah and his family and all the animals were in the ark for over a year!

Did you know… before the flood, animals were not afraid of people! Thank goodness, or those elephants would have been difficult to load. After they left the ark, God caused them to fear humans.

Did you know… the rainbow that appeared after the flood was the very first one!

A B C D E F
G H I J K L M
N O P Q R S T
U V W X Y Z

A long time ago, the earth was prosperous and full of people. But the people were wicked and mean. Their sinful thoughts and actions made God very sad, so He decided He would send a great flood to cover the whole earth.

ALLIGATOR

BABOON

COW

But one man, Noah, was special to God because he was good and kind. He loved God very much and did his best to do what was right and to teach his children to obey God too. God wanted to keep Noah and his family safe from the flood.

Dove

ELEPHANT

FROG

God told Noah to build a big boat called an ark. He told Noah to make the ark tall and wide, with lots of room inside.

God also told Noah that He would send him two of every animal, one boy and one girl of each – bugs and lizards and horses and birds. They would live with Noah in the ark, so he would need to gather lots of food to feed them.

GORILLA

IBIS

Noah did what God commanded and he put his whole family and all of the many animals into the ark. Then God shut the door and sealed them in. Knowing that Noah and his family and the animals were safe, God caused it to rain for many, many days and many, many nights.

Jay

Kangaroo

LION

The long rainstorm covered the whole earth with water and lifted the heavy ark off the ground and up toward the sky. There was so much rain that even the mountains were covered by the flood; but Noah and his family and all the animals were safe inside the ark.

MOUSE

NIGHT HERON

OWL

God did not forget Noah and He sent a mighty wind to blow the waters away. Slowly the waters disappeared from the earth and after one hundred fifty days the ark came to rest on the top of a mountain.

PANDA

QUAIL

RABBIT

Noah opened one of the ark's windows and released a bird to look for land. The bird always came back because there was no place for it to roost.

SQUIRREL

TIGER

URSUS

Ursus is the scientific name for a bear.

One day, when Noah sent a dove out to fly, it came back to him with an olive branch in its beak. And the next time Noah set the dove free, it flew away and did not come back. Noah looked out from the window and saw that the ground was dry.

Vulture

WOLF

XIAO

We didn't have a good "X"
animal so we used our dog Xiao.

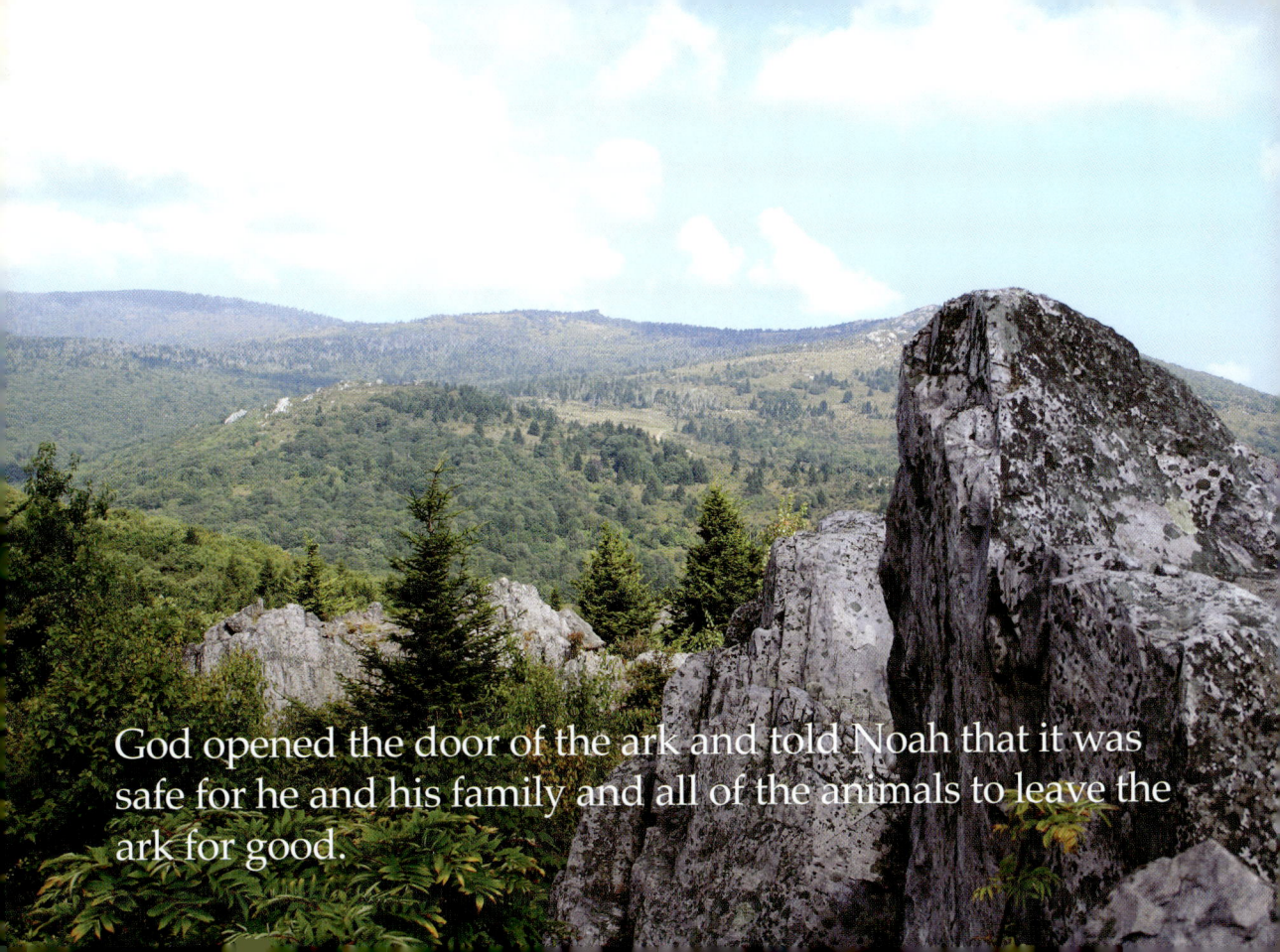

God opened the door of the ark and told Noah that it was safe for he and his family and all of the animals to leave the ark for good.

YAK

ZEBRA

God was very pleased
that Noah had obeyed Him.
He made a promise to Noah
and all of the living things that He
would never flood the whole earth
again. God created a rainbow to appear
in the heavens whenever it rained so that
no one would forget His promise. And Noah
and his sons and daughters and the birds and
horses and lizards and bugs looked up at the
colorful sky and began their new lives.

-THE END-

HANNAH T. WRIGHT
Hannah T. Wright is a typewriter enthusiast and professional worrier with an all-consuming passion for the written word. She has been reading and writing for as long as she can remember and finished her first Dickens novel before she learned to ride a bike at age 9 ... much to her parents' chagrin. She currently resides in North Carolina with her clever engineer husband Jason and their guinea pig, Hemingway.

MARK O. VOGEL
Since he was a small child, Mark has been fascinated by the art of photography. However, like adults often do, instead of pursuing his passion and a life of certain poverty, he chose to languish in a spacious corner corporate office. Now, on his off days he is making up for lost time and missed photographs. His favorite subjects are animals, plants, architecture and his family. Mark lives in Statesville, North Carolina with his wife and two sons (and within driving distance of his married daughter).

You can see more of Mark's photos in his first book entitled "Knock and the Door Will be Opened" which combines inspiring biblical quotations with beautiful companion images.